# WHERE COULD THE ANIMALS BE?

# THERE ARE **FOURTEEN** ANIMALS, WILD AND FREE...

# I WONDER WHERE THEY'RE HIDING, LET'S GO AND SEE!

# This is RONNIE REINDEER

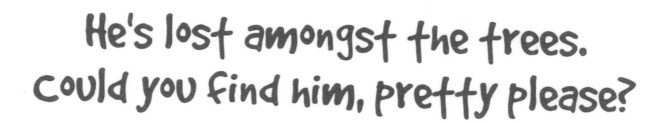

He's lost amongst the trees.
Could you find him, pretty please?

# FREDDY FISH

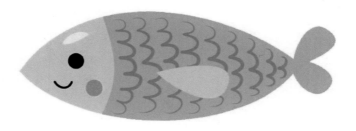

has scales, bright and blue.
Where can he be,
I haven't got a clue!

# This is
# MILLIE MOUSE

Where could she be?
She's smaller than an elephant
but larger than a flea!

find
# FINLEY THE FOX

if you'd be so kind.
He's a crafty fox,
so he might be hard to find!

# This is
# DONNY DUCK

He loves to quack.
He's got a brother called Katie and
a sister called Jack!

# Where's OLLY THE OWL?

He's very bright.
He sleeps all day,
then he comes out at night!

This is

# BECKY the BUTTERFLY

She's very rare.
She loves flying in the air!

I know he must be around.
So is

# GORDON THE GOAT

anywhere to be found?

Here's

# PADDY THE POOCH

he's a shy little dog.
He won't say ribbit, because Paddy's
not a frog!

# POLLY THE PARROT

loves to squawk and screech.
Her favourite place is a
nice sunny beach!

Here's

# TIMMY TORTOISE

He isn't very fast.
He tried to win a race,
but sadly he came last!

Her best friend is a cat.
Can you find

# RITA THE RABBIT

...she's wearing a scarf and a hat!

He's not a cat,
he's also not a dog.
Can you find

# FRANKIE THE FROG?

# Here's
# LISA LEOPARD

She's very quick.
She's also yellow,
just like a baby chick!

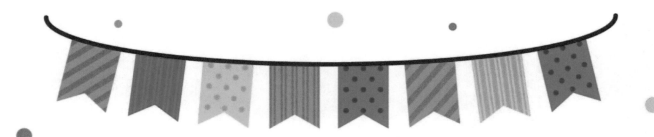

# WELL DONE!

You found all
the animals,
each and every one!

# THE END!

# Find us on Amazon!

Discover all of the titles available in our store;
including these below...

Made in the USA
Columbia, SC
29 November 2018